Albert Labbett's

CREDITON COLLECTION

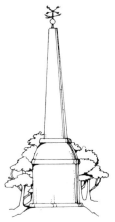

Albert Labbett.

OBELISK PUBLICATIONS

ACKNOWLEDGEMENTS

I am greatly indebted to so many people for supplying the photographs in this book, that I dare not try to list them all for fear of leaving someone out! I trust that everyone involved will accept my thanks, but I would like to say a special 'thank you' to Reg & Vi Botterell for reproducing and mounting the photographs.

I should like to dedicate this book to all my grandchildren hoping that they will preserve my collection of Crediton and district photographs for future Crediton generations.

Other Obelisk Publications

Around & About the Haldon Hills, Chips Barber
The Lost City of Exeter, Chips Barber
Diary of a Dartmoor Walker, Chips Barber
Adventure Through Red Devon, Raymond B Cattell
An Exeter Boyhood, Frank Retter
The Torbay Book, Chips Barber
Under Sail through South Devon & Dartmoor, R B Cattell
The Great Walks of Dartmoor, Terry Bound
Ide, Bill Rowland
Diary of a Devonshire Walker, Chips Barber
Rambling in the Plymouth Countryside, Lister & Woolley
The Great Little Dartmoor Book, Chips Barber
Tales of the Unexplained in Devon, Judy Chard
The Great Little Exeter Book, Chips Barber
The DevonAir Book of Family Walks, Chips Barber
Running in Devon, John Legge
Memories of Newton Abbot, Elsie Townsend

First Published in 1987 by Obelisk Publications,
2 Church Hill, Pinhoe, Exeter, Devon
Printed in Great Britain by Penwell Ltd, Parkwood, Callington, Cornwall.
C Albert Labbett 1987

The centre of Crediton was largely rebuilt following the great fire of 1743. It started in the region just to the left of this photo. At that time High Street was divided into three parts known as Narrow Street (from the green to 55 High Street), from there to Market Street it was called Broad Street, then to where the original road shot up to Park Street was the Market (there was no Union Road at that period). In those days the shops were simply stalls in the centre of the road, and most goods were kept in barrels. When gas lighting was established throughout the town, there were 64 lamp standards!

The name of Cox has been over a butcher's shop for 120 years. It started with James Cox, butcher of Morchard Bishop, who married Louise Horrell of Moor Farm in 1860. Later they moved to 8 Market Street, Crediton where James died at the early age of 49. In 1894 his widow bought 15/16 High Street and carried on the business with the help of her sons. She was succeeded in 1907 by Bert, her youngest son until his own retirement in 1935. The business then went to his nephews, Ned Cox and Wilfred Southcott.

The Green suffered the loss of its railings for the war munitions. In the 1880s it was an open space and fairs were held here. Right in the middle of the Green is the base of a cross which stood in the road at the bottom of St Saviours Way. Nobody knows where the shaft of the cross went. Under the base of the cross is a spring called "The Litterburn" which ran down through the town. When the town sewer was constructed the spring was fed into the sewer. William Bradley and John Roberts, 'scavengers', who died in 1711 and 1714, had the unenviable task of urging dead cats, dogs, vermin and town refuse along the open drains into the Litterburn.

This old thatched cottage at Blagdon Terrace was situated on the old main road to Barnstaple, that went via Sandford, Morchard Bishop, Black Dog and South Molton. The two people, one each side of the front gate, could be Jack Tuckett and his wife. The cottage was disposed of in a most unusual way—it was demolished and pushed down the well in the rear courtyard! The well is now capped and is situated by the front door of a more modern house, owned by Mr Lee who called it 'United House' after Crediton United Football Club.

This was known as the Red House and was located at the junction of Landscore and Western Road. The miller is unloading sacks of flour for the bakers from an old covered wagon of the 1880s. Earlier, in 1723, the main highway was by way of Landscore, whilst Western Road was merely a back lane. A map of 1765 shows the lane did not reach Western Lodge and nor did Alexandra Road (Turnagain Lane). At this time Widow Roach owned the ground in front of this house and Tuckfield, of Shobrooke Park, owned the land on which the house stood.

Prideaux, who lived at Lower Westwood in 1520, settled a right of way dispute with Arundel of Yeoton (Uton) by an amicable arbitration. The footbridge was constructed for passage over an open stream that crossed the road, but is now piped beneath it as, during heavy rains, the road was often flooded. This stream divided Crediton Urban and Rural Districts. Ern Parker owned the Smithy on this side of the footbridge. On the chimney above the Smithy is a sign (unknown) with a date of 1640. Westwood was the old hunting lodge of the Bishops of Exeter many years ago.

About 1750 the manor house on the left was the largest house in the west town. It was three storeys high and had three attic windows. It boasted an impressive front entrance with two ornamental pillars standing well into the street as we know it today. At the time there was no Searle Street or Market Street, only North Street on the north side of the High Street. A large fire in 1769, which spread from Bowden Hill to Back Lane (Parliament Street), destroyed more than 200 houses. Positioned on the right of Parliament Street was Grove the Baker's shop which later transferred its business to the High Street.

This scene was taken from Fountain Corner, at the junction of East and Charlotte Streets, after the great storm on 3rd March 1891 when the town came to a standstill for a week. The snow in the High Street was six feet deep and a trench was cut in the middle of the road for people to gain access to collect bread. The householders still had to dig themselves out to reach the main trench. The Fountain, opened by Lady Audrey Buller, comprised of two large horse drinking bowls either side of a small hand operated spout for people. Unfortunately a car crashed into it one morning and smashed it beyond repair.

Fordton

On 27th September 1621 John Prouze purchased Fordton Barton from Sir William Killigrew for £250, the annual rent being 40 shillings. At a later date Honor Prouze willed Fordton Barton and the residue of her estate to the Rev John Stacey, who may have been the object of her affections. The poor chap was fatally injured by a fall from his horse whilst on his way home from Exeter one day. The main road from Crediton to Exeter was via Four Mills Road, Fordton and Venny Tedburn. The cottages on the right were severely damaged by the floods of the 1960s and were later pulled down.

High Street, Crediton.

The High Street of 1930. Note the number of shops compared with the offices and building societies of today. Young lads re-enacted the Oxford and Cambridge boat race using matches in the gutter on the left. It stretched along most of the south side of the High Street to the top of North Street. Another popular game was 'fag cards'. Nearly all cigarette packets had cards inside them. The boys stood one of them upright against a house, then knelt on the kerb and flicked their cards, trying to knock the upright one down. Whoever succeeded collected the cards which had missed the target.

Resurfacing Charlotte Street. The bowler-hatted man was Billo Lake, the foreman, who lived at Landscore. Charlotte Street was named after Mrs Buller of Downes House, the street being located entirely on Buller property. The building of Clarence Villa, midway along its length, caused the closure of the centuries old 'Canon Walk' that passed through Queens Court to East Street. The Canon Walk went from the top of White Hart Hill to the church. An act of Parliament in 1836 received royal assent for the improvement of Crediton—before then Charlotte Street did not exist as a thoroughfare.

The house behind the lad on the right, at the bottom of Cockle's Lane, is believed to be that of the Davie Family, treasurer of the Collegiate Church, and one of the oldest houses in Crediton. The chantry, with the iron rail in front, has a tunnel in the cellar, the entrance to which is now bricked up, but it is high enough to walk along upright. It leads towards the churchyard to a crypt and possibly links up with the tunnel from Union Road. The chantry tunnel was found to have some very slender stalactites hanging from the roof, but they were broken off when the house was opened for inspection after the death of Parry Jones in 1953. In 1907 in Dean Street, a fatal accident befell John Drew when a cob wall fell on him.

Here we see Frederick John Helmore, his wife and baby, Bert, in about 1890, outside his Union Road office located near "The Steps" by the iron railings. The office moved to Church View in 1900 and then to the present address of 103 High Street. Helmores are believed to be the oldest established firm of auctioneers and estate agents in the country, having now been in practice for over 255 years. Bert joined his father in partnership in the 1920s. Alan Stoyle (Snr) joined the firm in 1924 as articled clerk and became a partner in 1947. His two sons, John and Alan (Jnr) now run the practice.

Left: The Seven Stars Inn was at 115 High Street and is now a printer's shop. The inn was twice destroyed by fire, in 1743 and again in 1858. Three thatchers, of the Crediton Fire Brigade, were specially rewarded for their efforts in making a fire-break in the thatched roof, thus saving the Oat Sheaf Inn. It was re-erected largely in brick except for the cob skittle alley which today houses the printer's press. In humid weather it is possible, despite the numerous coats of whitewash, to discern its original sign proclaiming its status as an inn. Mr Welch was the landlord in 1778 and Mr Miller was the landlord in 1850. 'Time' was called for the last time in 1909.

Centre: This is the old Swan Inn, now Ivor Coram's shoe shop. According to the London Gazette of 1794, Simon Lane, the landlord, was confined to the debtor's prison in St Thomas, Exeter. The names of the inns were coupled with those of the publicans for the first time in 1783, for submission to the licencing authorities.

Right: The Oat Sheaf Hotel, formerly a cob and thatched tenement, is said to have had eaves so low that they could be touched by the up-stretched hand. It was rebuilt in 1885 and owes its corner position to the making of Searle Street when adjacent cottages were pulled down to make way for the road. The horse chestnut tree was cut down in the mid 1920s to make way for an electricity pole and overhead cables. W.H. Blatchford, a former landlord of the inn, is named on the Crediton War Memorial.

The Angel, one of the oldest hostelries, dated from the reign of Henry VII in 1504 when "Le Angel" stood in the name of John Wevyll. The church-warden's accounts of 1557 stated that "on the sixth day and second year of the reignes of our sovereign Lord and Lady Kynge Phylpp and Quene Mary the XII Governors of the Corporation of the Churches of Crediton and Mr Dowreyshe met together here at Crediton at the saigne of the Angell." Outside the Angel Inn there is a deep gutter which was continuous, without any drain, from the Green to North Street. It was flushed from the spring at the Green.

This is the scene of the April Great Market about 1920. The cattle, all Red Devons, stretched from the Green to the War Memorial. These fairs or markets started with a grant from Henry III to the Bishop of Exeter. A later grant from Edward I increased the fairs to two a year, the first being the cattle market of the spring, the second, in autumn, was concerned with sales of corn, leather and wool. In later years, swings, roundabouts and many amusements were held at the Green and also in the main street.

CREDITON APRIL MARKET. 1911.

This is the parade of the stallions. It occurred in the afternoon of the April Great Market. The cattle, sold or not, were driven away and the stallions were paraded from the stables of the market house, and up Market Street to the High Street for inspection by local farmers. Small boys of the town always had their sticks which was part of the scene in those days. One pastime was to climb the gas lamp standards and swing on the cross arm. It's hard to spot anyone without a cap or a bowler hat!

This is the Whit Sunday church procession of 1911 passing the frontage of the congregational church. Four old thatched cottages once stood on the space where the lamp and railings are. These were demolished to make way for the chapel built in 1865. Channon did the masonry, Heathman the iron and woodwork, Hall and Thomas the painting, glazing and decorating, at the total cost of £2,000. The original church, not far away, had its entrance between No 107 and 108 High Street. In the house, right of the entrance, lived Bruce Adams who owned the tannery. This was stituated at the lower end of Waresfoot Drive. No 101 was occupied by C.J. Bicknell, Tailor.

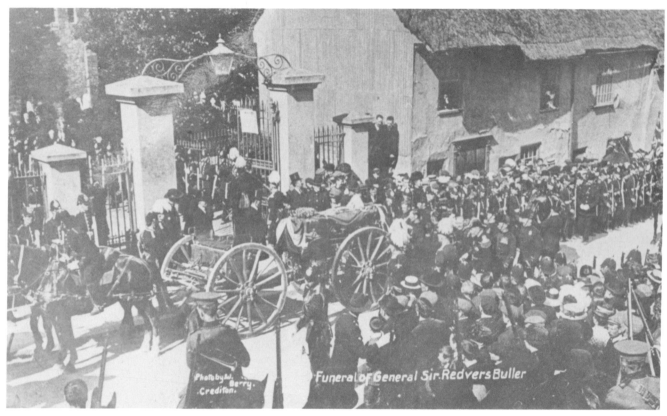

The funeral of General Sir Redvers Buller, VC buried in Crediton Churchyard in 1908. His coffin is on a gun carriage followed by one of his chargers. They were called Biffin and Ironmonger and the General's boots were reversed in the stirrups of one of these horses. Beside the gun carriage paced Field Marshall Lord Wolseley and other distinguished officers. It was escorted by two squadrons of the Royal Devon Yeomanry, 3rd Batt. Rifle Brigade, 2nd Devons and 80 Petty Officers of the RNVR. Other troops lined the route. Guns of a field battery, R A in position on Down Heyn, boomed out a last salute. General Buller died at his home, Downes, just outside the town.

In this photograph the crowds are waiting outside the Town Hall to hear the declaration of the result of the 1924 election of the Torrington Division. George Lambert of Spreyton stood for the Liberals and Cedric Drewe of Drogo Castle for the Conservatives. The latter had a majority of 654 votes. Just left of the policeman on the right is Bill Discombe with his young son Gilbert (no hat). Also to be seen are brothers Bert and Dick Labbett, hands in pockets and wearing soft caps. Harry Ayres was the landlord of the White Swan in the background.

Peace Day in Crediton. This shows a nursing association of the First World War outside the Ship Hotel. Many buildings in the town were used as hospitals, Western Lodge, The Liberal Club, and Cherry and Symes Garage being just some of them. The shelter at upper deck was built for the wounded service men of that war, at the instigation of Miss Adams of Crediton. Shops left to right of photo, Yelland (Outfitter), Frank Smith (Draper), Lock (Seed and Corn Merchant), Horrell and Son (Ironmongers), Bragg (Wine and Spirit Merchant), Street (Chemists).

Celebrating Coronation Day on 26th June 1902. Liberal donations were made for festivities and entertainments and tables were spread along the High Street for a fare of roast beef, plum pudding, cider and beer. The double fronted shop of John Mann was registered in 1840 as a place of religious worship. The organ was played by John Mann at meetings of the Plymouth Brethren. Some years later Mrs Mann built the Gospel Hall which is now Mitchell the Baker. An advertisement of 1891 describes the coffee palace and refreshment rooms of 124 High Street with good beds, cooked beef and ham sent out at 1s 6d per lb.

This scene is of the Peace Celebrations in Crediton in 1919. This photo is taken from No 4 High Street looking towards Union Road. The building on the extreme left was part of the old telephone exchange. At that time No 142 High Street was Newcombe and Son (House furnishers), No 143 was E.E. Tuck (Outfitter), No 144 was W.J. Lake (Dairy) and at No 144A was R. Sprague the town crier.

This wonderful picture shows a merry crowd enjoying an afternoon cup of tea in Park Street, which was at one time the main road from Exeter through the town. Note the archway opposite the entrance to Barnfield, just below that were the two shops of Heale the Baker and Sprague the Grocer. Cockles Rise is now situated behind this group of people. The character seated in the centre was the rag and bone man, Mr Yarde, seated to his right is Mary Ann Nicholes and on her right is Mrs Phillips. Standing at the rear with the child is Nell Osbourne and her mother. In the doorway Mrs Setter can be seen with her young son Harold.

CREDITON FLOWER SHOW SPORTS, 1914

This Crediton Flower Show and Sports tooks place in 1914 at Palace Meadow, now Meadow Gardens. The refreshment and beer tents were always part of these fetes. In later years the British Legion held their annual sports at the recreation field in Exhibition Road. I recall being paid 7s 6d (38p) for winning the mile. As 5s (25p) was my spending money for the week, five minutes of running was well worth the effort! A sprinter named Cox, who came from Exeter, would attend all the local village sports days to earn himself additional pay packets.

This shows the Fair, held at the Green, about 1880. The swing boats in the picture were Morgan's swings still operating at village fetes until recent times. A sketch of the Green about 1750 shows thatched cottages all along the front of it. In 1860 the town improvement commissioners, in a representation made to the Lord of the Manor, regarding the undue prolongation of the annual fair, pointed out that it was being strung out over several days whereas in the past it was held for three days only. The final day was formerly know as "bull-baiting day". We can only surmise that, in those early days, bull baiting took place here.

Buller Park.

People's Park was laid out in the old rack field as a memorial to James Wentworth Buller who was buried at Exwick in 1822. He was admitted to the freedom of the City of Exeter, and for many years was Whig Member of Parliament for North Devon. One individual referred to him as "the great Crediton snob"—he was never seen in public in other than frock coat and top hat. The entrance to the park at that time was by a footpath from the High Street. By the mid 1850s Searle Street was made along the same route as the path. In the 1928 street directory there were only three houses in People's Park Road, "St Boniface", "The Gables" and "The Orchard".

In Vicorian times Crediton Working Men's Club purchased a number of velocipedes. John Dicker made his own from a round table top. The next improvement was the penny farthing and John Mann, the Grocer, had one. A.L. Stoyle and F. Sprague pedalled from Crediton to London and back on their 'cushion' tyre cycles, the first stop being Winchester. Before and after the last war most workers would either walk or cycle to work and to the local villages around Crediton, cycles being the most common means of transport.

left
The flags and decorations which adorn 18—19 High Street are hung out to celebrate Coronation Day on 26th June 1902 when Edward VII was crowned. S. Baker's Drapery & Millinery Stores were well known for their dress and mantel making, "perfect fit and style guaranteed" and were also noted for both their French and English millinery. Funerals were also completely furnished.

centre
This is the Crediton Fire Brigade, circa 1890, pictured at Russ Cottages, Threshers Road. On the extreme left is Dr Heygate who was Chief Officer. The windows and doors remain largely the same today.

right
This shows another important ceremony, the opening of the Town and Hamlets' War Memorial on which 137 victims from the First World War are named, in addition to another 40 from the Second World War. The list includes many men from the Devonshire Regiment.

This is Crediton Town Band taken outside Fordton House, owned by Mr Authers, during a fete in 1953. Back row left to right: Robert Powlesland, Michael Deem, Melvin Hansford, Eddie Darch, Bill Gilbert, Richard Powlesland, Brian Deem. Middle Row: Bill Stoneman, Charlie Mogridge, Ron Matten, Peter Setter, Jack Tuckett, Len Edwards, George Vicary. Front Row: Ron Hamlin, Horace Grant, Fred Harvey, Art Setter (Bandmaster), Gerald Mogridge, Ron Howard, Harold Setter. Traditionally the first outside engagement of the year was on the Saturday evening after the April Great Market.

This day trip to Weymouth, for the staff of Ernest Jackson and Co, took place on 19th July 1929. This firm was well known for manufacturing blackcurrant flavoured lozenges and licorice imps. The main supplier of blackcurrant was farmer George Mortimer of Uton. The bus driver was Bill Copp and his passengers were George Andrews, Bob Webber, Kit Snell, Freda Chudley, Alice Snell, Violet Coles, Edith Coles, May Steer, Roy Elston, Miss Chamberlain, Flo Nott, Mr Bubear, Bert Bubear, Ida Chilcot, Mr Searle, Mr Hodge, Mr Mutley, Mr Thomson, Clara James and Emily Pike.

This dramatic photograph depicts the burnt out shells of the three cottages opposite the White Hart Hotel in Exeter Road. The fire, which happened on a Sunday in 1935, completely gutted these thatched cottages. Firemen Albert Kenshole had a lucky escape when his ladder broke whilst he was fighting the fire. Fortunately he fell outside the blazing building and suffered only minor injuries. The occupants at the time were R. Vanstone at No 1, C. Bastin, the basketmaker in No 1a and F. Steer at No 2 which is now a showroom.

This fine body of men is the Crediton Fire Brigade of 1906 outside the brigade's headquarters, now the Conservative Club. The smart men with lovely brass helmets and white breeches that I can identify are Bob Johns, Noah Balsom, William Boddy, Jack Kelland, Tom Clay and Albert Kenshole, in the 2nd, 3rd, 4th, 7th, 8th, and 9th positions respectively, from the left. The bugle boy, Reg Yelland, lived down Mann's Court in the High Street. The Bridgade's next station was located where the library now stands. After this they moved on the North Street and then to their present position in Market Street.

Crediton Fire Brigade's Carnival entry outside the Conservative Club. This horse drawn fire engine would lead the carnival procession. The large cotton waste ball suspended on a chain would be soaked in paraffin and set alight, being one mass of flame. Also about 20 paraffin torches were placed about to light the wagon. Included in this photograph are officers Johns and Discombe, Waggoner Tottle, Bugler Spotty Elston, firemen Noah Balsom and Albert Kenshole. Lack of water was the biggest problem years ago. In 1859 nine thatched cottages in St Laurence's Green were just left to burn themselves out as no water was available. As a result, Richard Gay, the uninsured owner living in North Street, hanged himself from a beam in his bedroom.

This is Crediton's post office staff of 1905. Mrs Susannah Guins who was landlady of the Ship Inn was appointed sub-postmaster in 1770 at £3 per annum. William Bradford was a Victorian roundsman who did 20 miles per day, six days a week for 44 years—a total distance of over a quarter of a million miles—further than Crediton to the moon! His exceptional record was made complete by the fact that his total absences from work amounted to only 15 days in all that time. It was not until 1850 that postal workers had a free Sunday.

In 1853 trains left Exeter at the following times on their journeys to Crediton: 4.30am, 9.30am, 11.00am 1.15pm, 3.10pm, 4.20pm, 6.35pm and 9.15pm. The royal mail for Bideford left Crediton on the 4.30am train. The "Queen" or "Ruby" (horse carriage) left Crediton for Barnstaple at 1.15pm. The "Hero" (horse carriage) left Crediton for Bideford via Torrington at 3.30pm. Bideford was the mail port for America from London. Single fares by train to Exeter were 1st class 1s (5p), 2nd class 9d (3p) 3rd class 4d. Rates for cattle, horses, carriages, coal, lime and goods were given, on application, at the station.

In 1920 hansom cabs were for hire at Crediton railway station. These awaited passengers off the train from Exeter. Some of the horses in the queue would also have pulled the fire engine. The old cabbie in the foreground was Bob Brinley who was often the worse for drink. Not only youngsters but older passengers also played jokes on him. On one occasion, coming up White Hart Hill, a passenger jumped out of Bob's carriage and hopped into a speedier cab coming up behind. When poor Bob arrived at the destination he found his cab empty and, on knocking on the door of his destination, was totally dumbfounded to find his passenger opening the door!

This is one of the earliest photographs of Crediton and shows tanners and curriers outside Adams' Tanyard entrance about 1850 to 1860. It was founded by Edward Adams in 1792 and was the last tanyard in the town, closing in the 1960s when Bruce Adams was the owner. Oak bark is being unloaded from the large covered wagon. The hides would pickle in the oak bark of the tan pits for twelve months, but bark was later replaced by chemicals which cured the hides in a matter of weeks. The oak bark previously used in the tan pits was added to logs and kept many homes warm but always the smell of the tan pits filled the cottages. Another use for the used oak bark was to spread it on the road if a person was very ill, greatly reducing the noise of the iron wheels of the passing carts.

This is a photo of Samuel Gimblett and his workers at the rear of No 111 High Street, connected to nearby Adams' Tannery by trolley lines to convey leather to shoemakers' benches. Samuel Gimblett was a Cornishman who settled in Crediton about 1868. He initiated the round table method of mass production. For his workers he provided a club and social hall with a floor laid for roller skating.

This shows workers outside Ernest Jackson and Co, Union Road. The rails outside were removed during the last war for munitions as were the church rails. The building was erected for Elston's boot and shoe firm and at one time turned out hundreds of pairs of heavy boots a week for African miners. The firm closed down early in 1914 which was unfortunate as, had it held on for a few months longer, the demand for army boots during the war would have kept the firm in business. The building has now been turned into flats. In the cellar of the ivy covered house is an entrance to a tunnel leading to the churchyard.

A scene outside Hayward's School, East Street, Crediton about 1880. The interest from money in Sir Roland Hayward's trust accumulated over many years and the school was built at a cost of £3,000. The contractor was John Mason of Exeter and the architect was Mr Hayward. Ernest Bevan, a former Foreign Secretary, was a scholar at the school until he left in 1890. The old thatched cottages on the left have been pulled down for the enlargement of the churchyard. The Ring o'Bells and Prince Fredrick, at one time public houses, stood there. Around the corner in Church Lane stood "The Plymouth Inn" which later transferred its premises to Dean Street.

The Grammar School, Crediton. In the second year of the reign of Queen Elizabeth I the school became Queen Elizabeth's Free Grammar School and its first master was Christopher Bodleigh. In the twelfth year of the Queen's reign the lady chapel of the church was used for the school. In 1852 it moved to the new buildings on the green. In summer the teaching hours were 7.30am to 9.00am, and 10.00am to 1.00pm, 2.45pm to 5.00pm and winter 9.00am to 12 noon and 2.00pm to 5.00pm. For lighting the boys had to bring their own candles. All examination questions were written in Latin and Greek.

A view of Queen Elizabeth's Grammar School taken from the top of Stoney Park Lane ('Tin Pot' as old people of Kirton would call it). The building at the rear of the school is the old gymnasium. On the spot where the front entrance of the school is located once stood a row of weavers' cottages. These were demolished, as were the cottages half way up St Martins Lane, to make way for the building of the school. Note that the bell tower on the roof has disappeared. The rural background scene has now been turned into a mostly developed area.

Miss Westcott's class of 1928 at the Old Landscore school, Crediton. Although I have not been able to identify everyone in the picture, it has proved possible to name the following: Back row, left to right: Sid Bicknell, Jack Denner, Bert Loosemore, Reg Salter, Laurie Labbett, Edgar Courtney, Ron Turner, Albert Tonkin, Miss Westcott. Middle Row: —, Kathleen Parr, Kenneth Parr, Muriel Robinson, Violet Seldon, M. Giles, —, Phyllis Burden, Doris Hill, —. Front Row: Bert Norton, Ron Steer, Len Milford, Molly Deem, Betty Rippon, May Avery, Ron Hopper, Doris Burrows. The Headmistress at that time was Mrs Ash.

This is the original golf course at Uton, Crediton as it was in the 1920s. The club professional, Mr A. Whittaker, is shown putting on one of the nine greens. The club was formed in the spring of 1923. The nine hole course was 2,540 yards long and was situated a little over a mile from the town. Local information from 1928 describes it as in good playing order with a pavilion, and every convenience for the use of members. The professional was always at the course and supplied members with all their various requisites. There were nearly 100 playing members. The subscriptions were three guineas per annum for gentlemen and two guineas per annum for ladies.

This photo was taken at the recreation field late 1940s. Standing, left to right: C. Hulland, S. Vigers, H. Blean, G. Oliver, Fred Bennett (Groundsman), Curruthers, —. Sitting: Parry Jones, (Umpire), A. Shape, R. Roach, John Symes (President), Dr Jackson (Capt), F. Bourne, Dr Sherren, C. Luxton. Probably about 1896 was the most successful period for local cricket when Kirton played such seasoned elevens as Taunton Town. They fielded such fine players as S.J.W. Woods the bowler, and J.B. Challen, Headmaster of Crediton Grammar School who both played for the Somerset County Team. Sadly no team exists today, the nearest being at Creedy Park and Shobrooke Park.

Crediton Rugby Football Club was formed in 1878 and originally the playing area was at the recreation field in Exhibition Road. The present ground and club house is situated across the road not far from the old ground. In April 1924 the club won the Devon Junior Cup beating Salcombe, at Teignmouth, by a try and a penalty goal to nil. The team that day was G. Burrows, W. Snell, A.C.T. Blease, H. Setter, F. Welham, G. Tuckett, F. Tuckett, W.S. Boddy, B. Perkins, W. Vincent, L. Wollacott, C. Burridge, S. Labbett, F. Parr, A.B. Gay, F. Steer. Crediton won it again in 1947 beating Buckfastleigh by 3 points to nil at Exeter. The team was C. Haydon, W. Lee, F. Tuckett, A. Labbett, R. Turner, T. Powlesland, D. Cornall, D. Prettejohns, R. Dyer, N. Littlejohns, J. Crooke, T. Cullis, D. Trick, L. Boddy, T. Lee.

The Crediton United team of 1911-12. After the Second World War the present Crediton United was formed by an amalgamation of members of the pre-war clubs of Crediton Rangers, Jackson's Centurions and old Haywardians. A new ground was provided at Newcombes playing fields and the club played there until 1976. The following honours have been won: Senior Div I Championship 1963 and 1967, Senior Div B Championships 1971, Junior Div 3 1949 and 1950, Okehampton Challenge Cup 1973 and 75, Whitbread Flowers Cup 1979, Geary Cup 2nd XI 1985, Lidden Cup 3rd XI 1985. Only three players can be identified in this photo, sitting first left is S. Labbett, his father Jack Labbett on the extreme right and Art Setter (wearing a bowler hat). S. Labbett also played rugby for Crediton and Devon.

This is Spurway Almshouses at the Lynch in Park Street, one of the oldest buildings in Crediton still occupied to the present day. They were built about 1555 at the bequest of Humphrey Spurway, a clothier of Kirton. Humprey Spurway, in his will dated 1st February 1555, gave to his wife the rent of his lands, lying within the Parish of Witheridge, for her life, and after her death to remain forever to the almshouses at Crediton. He directed that after the aforesaid almshouses should be built, William Shilston and Robert Hooke should put in four poor folk. The only 'fire mark sign' in the town is on the wall in the centre of the almshouses.

The Unitarian Chapel was at the Lynch, Park Street, the licence for which is dated 1731. "It is certified and recorded at the present sessions that the house newly built on part of Bray's field in the west town and borough of Crediton is appointed a place of worship." Bray's Field, it is supposed, was part of Christopher Saunder's bequest of 1715 which included the row of thatched cottages below the chapel, which older Kirtonians should remember. The chapel was the largest single room cob building in Devon. It has since been demolished and old people's flats have been built on the site.

The church of the Holy Cross looking towards the Church Street entrance. Crediton Church was built in the form of a cross. During the terrible plague of 1571 there were 540 deaths which accounted for more than a quarter of the population. So frequent were the burials that it was impossible for one man to undertake them all and Bishop Bradbridge granted a licence to William Wattes, one of the parish clerks, to help bury the dead. The church was provided with a dog-whipper, whose duty was to drive out dogs, and sometimes to arouse sleeping members of the congregation! The death of Philip Strong, dog-whipper, is recorded in the register of 1628.

The installation of new seating at the church. Down each side of the nave a stone bench runs under the windows which, in the middle ages, was the only seating for the congregation. It was intended to serve as a resting place for the old folk, while the younger members knelt or stood during the mass. In 1580 the choir was filled with "seages" or seats. In later years some of the leading families of the town and district had their own pews installed.

This photograph of Mr Stacey was taken in 1912 outside Elmfield, Fordton, Crediton. This fine pair of horses pulled a Victorian carriage, a light low four-wheeled vehicle and sat two passengers facing the horses. The livery was the same colour as that of the coach—green and black. 'Elmfield' was built for Dr Edward Yarde. Mr. Stacey was also the coachman for another doctor called Evans and today the house is occupied by yet another, Doctor Forbes. It was one of the first houses to be lit by 64 jets of gas, the same number that were used to light all the streets of Crediton!

Creedy Park near Crediton. The Davy family once lived in Dean Street, Crediton. This view is of the east end of the old house which was completely gutted by fire in November 1915. John Davy 1541—1611 was three times Mayor of Exeter. At Creedy Park he entertained Don Antonio who was driven into exile by Philip of Spain, having sanctuary there for three months owing to his ill health. Queen Elizabeth gave Davy the right to clothe his servants in blue and gold and to use the Kingfisher as his crest The hounds of the hunt of Yarde of Trobridge invaded Creedy Park, and Sir William, objecting to this, built a wall around most of the estate to keep the hounds at bay. The estate was finally broken up in 1975.

Shobrooke Park House, the former home of the Shelley family. It was burnt down during the last war when it was being used as a school and two children lost their lives. A schoolboy had to run to Crediton to raise the alarm. This house was built for Hippesley-Tuckfield. The original house named 'Little Fulford' stood behind the present cricket pavilion. Here lived Lord Chief Justice Peryam who was knighted in 1593. He was keeper of the Queen's purse and sat at the trial of Mary Queen of Scots. He died in 1604 in Buckinghamshire and was brought home for burial in Crediton, amidst great pomp. Nearly all Kirton's population would have massed along the route from Little Fulford to the church.

Forches Bridge, Crediton.

This bridge, which was removed in 1969, was the link between two tree plantations on the Creedy Park estate. Three soldiers of a detachment stationed here in 1768 raped a woman near Forches. She identified them and they were sent for trial at Exeter. Found guilty, they were returned to the very spot of their crime and hanged. Three hundred years ago a Crediton woman committed suicide and, denied a christian burial, was committed to the earth at the four cross roads at Forches. This was a concession given by the church that outcasts were at least permitted a grave—and the crossroads was chosen because of it being a sign of the cross.

Shobrooke Village

The thatched houses of Shobrooke are much the same today as when this photo was taken in the 1920s. Part of the Red Lion Inn is just in the picture on the left. The field on the right is now School Close with an entrance opposite the Red Lion. One of the routes from Crediton to Exeter was via this village then to a ford of the River Exe at Rewe and then on to Exeter. The village is mentioned in 1288 when Thomas Lampreye of 'Shepbroke' was hanged for a matter not stated. Dr Laurence Bodley, Rector of Shobrooke, was brother of the famous Sir Thomas Bodley who founded the Bodleian library at Oxford.

Abraham Cann, a champion wrestler of England in 1827 came from the village of Colebrooke. In 1825 Cann won the Devon and Cornwall Championship beating Polkinghorne at Plymouth. He was then 30 years of age, stood 5'8", weighed 12 stone and was a man of immense strength. One contest was staged in London and the coach left the Bull Inn, Exeter. As there was no room for the wrestler on the coach, he said, "I'll go on my own feet". This he did, in stages, running a good deal of the way to collect a £20 bet for his exploit.

Coleford Village.

In the civil war period Coleford Village was on the main road from Crediton to Okehampton. Little has changed since this photograph was taken except for some of the thatches have been replaced by slate and the wheelwright's stone has since gone. King Charles once stood under the archway behind the lamp standard during the civil war (1642—1646) and reviewed his troops whilst passing through towards Okehampton. An army of 8,000, 500 horse and 500 dragoons with packhorses must have been quite a sight for the local population. Charles spent the night at Bow where a soldier was hanged for plundering.

BOW, DEVON.

The church is about two miles away, presumed to be the area of an early village 'Nymet Tracey'. Baron de Tracey, one of the Barons who killed Thomas A Becket, gave his name to this area. The name of Bow could be derived from the church of St Bartholemew, from the first, middle and last letter of Bartholemew. During the civil war, Sir Hardress Waller, en route for Plymouth, with two regiments, fought against the royalists at Bow. A mound on either side of Bow Bridge is said to cover the dead of that skirmish. In 1872 the favourite local sport was wrestling. Harris of Bow defeated Stone of Crediton. Bow became a village notorious for the robustness of their play, and were known as 'Bow Toughs'.